The Nation's #1 Educational Publisher

Grade 1
Word Builders

Vocabulary • Reading & Writing
A McGraw·Hill/Warner Bros. Workbook

Table of Contents

ABC Order 3	Homophones 21
ABC Order 4	Review 22
ABC Order 5	Progress Check 23
Review 6	Endings: -ed and -ing 24
Progress Check 7	Endings: -ed and -ing 25
Alphabetical Order 8	Endings: -ed and -ing 26
Alphabetical Order 9	Base Words and Endings 27
Alphabetical Order 10	Endings: -s and -es 28
Review 11	Endings: -s and -es 29
Progress Check 12	Endings: -s and -es 30
Guide Words 13	Endings: -er and -est 31
Antonyms 14	Endings: -er and -est 32
Antonyms 15	Endings: -er and -est 33
Synonyms 16	Review 34
Synonyms 17	Progress Check 35
Synonyms 18	Plurals: -s and -es 36
Homophones 19	Plurals: -s and -es 37
Homophones 20	Plurals: -s and -es 38

Table of Contents (continued)

Review	39
Progress Check	40
Adding 's	41
Adding 's	42
Adding 's	43
Review	44
Progress Check	45
Compound Words	46
Compound Words	47
Compound Words	48
Review	49
Progress Check	50
Contractions	51
Contractions	52
Contractions	53
Review	54
Progress Check	55
Prefixes	56
Prefixes	57
Prefixes	58
Suffixes	59
Suffixes	60
Suffixes	61
Review	62
Syllables	63
Progress Check	64
Answer Key	65

Credits:
McGraw-Hill Learning Materials Editorial/Production Team
Vincent F. Douglas, B.S. and M. Ed.
Tracy R. Paulus
Jennifer P. Blashkiw
Design Studio
Mike Legendre; Creativity On Demand

Warner Bros. Worldwide Publishing Editorial/Production Team
Michael Harkavy   Charles Carney
Paula Allen   Allen Helbig
Victoria Selover   Sara Hunter
Illustrators
Cover and Interior: Animated Arts!™

McGraw-Hill Consumer Products
A Division of The McGraw-Hill Companies

Copyright © 1999 McGraw-Hill Consumer Products.

Published by McGraw-Hill Learning Materials, an imprint of McGraw-Hill Consumer Products.

Printed in the United States of America. All rights reserved. Except as permitted under the United States Copyright Act, no part of this publication may be reproduced or distributed in any form or by any means, or stored in a database or retrieval system, without prior written permission from the publisher.

The McGraw-Hill Junior Academic Workbook Series and logo are trademarks of The McGraw-Hill Companies © 1999.

ANIMANIACS, characters, names, and all related indicia are trademarks of Warner Bros. © 1999.

Send all inquiries to:
McGraw-Hill Consumer Products
250 Old Wilson Bridge Road
Worthington, Ohio 43085

1-57768-231-9

ABC Order

Each letter has its own place in the alphabet.

a b c d e f g h i j k l m
n o p q r s t u v w x y z

Look at the letters in each box. In the blank, write the missing letter. The letters in each box should be in ABC order.

m n o	___ u ___ w
___ b ___ d	c ___ e
___ x y ___	___ p ___ r
j ___ l ___	___ ___ h i

3

ABC Order

a b c d e f g h i j k l m
n o p q r s t u v w x y z

Look at the letters in each box. Write the letters in ABC order.

mkl klm

poq ___

pon ___

srq ___

ghf ___

cba ___

zyx ___

hji ___

4

ABC Order

a b c d e f g h i j k l m
n o p q r s t u v w x y z

Look at the letters in each box. Write the letters in ABC order. The letters you write should form a word.

opm *mop*	edn _____
tih _____	ebg _____
bte _____	fyl _____
ofx _____	ton _____

5

 NAME

REVIEW

Write the missing letters to complete the alphabet.

a   b   c   ___   e

___   g   h   ___   j

___   l   m   ___   ___

p   ___   r   ___   t

___   v   ___   ___   y

Name

Progress Check

Look at the letters in each box. Write the letters in ABC order. The letters you write should form a word.

onw	now	obx	
t i f		cto	
t b i		mih	
o g t		f n i	

NAME _____

ALPHABETICAL ORDER

You can put words in alphabetical order by writing the first letter of each word in alphabetical order.

bed
play
yard

Read each set of words below. Then look at the first letter of each word to write the words in alphabetical order.

talk   bug   horse

1. bug
2. _____
3. _____

rain   feet   zoo

1. _____
2. _____
3. _____

egg   ice   apple

1. _____
2. _____
3. _____

dress   sun   noise

1. _____
2. _____
3. _____

8

Alphabetical Order

Read each set of words below. Then look at the first letter of each word to write the words in alphabetical order.

like   work   down

1. down
2. _____
3. _____

wet   miss   fun   ant

1. _____
2. _____
3. _____
4. _____

jump   can   stop

1. _____
2. _____
3. _____

yard   hen   bag   ox

1. _____
2. _____
3. _____
4. _____

NAME

ALPHABETICAL ORDER

When words begin with the same letter, use the second letters to put the words in alphabetical order.

dog
dish
draw

Read each set of words below. Write the words in alphabetical order.

ax   ask   and

1. and
2.
3.

give   gas   get

1.
2.
3.

sun   sack   song

1.
2.
3.

east   eye   egg

1.
2.
3.

Review

Read each set of words below. Then write the words in alphabetical order. You may have to look at the second letter in some words.

truck lock gate

1. gate
2. _____
3. _____

bake brake blue

1. _____
2. _____
3. _____

stay scrub shell slip

1. _____
2. _____
3. _____
4. _____

up pass know cow

1. _____
2. _____
3. _____
4. _____

PROGRESS CHECK

Read each set of words below. Then look at the first or second letter of each word to write the words in alphabetical order.

crab   car   clock

1. car
2.
3.

wash   ring   need

1.
2.
3.

pet   bird   duck   cat

1.
2.
3.
4.

old   one   off   open

1.
2.
3.
4.

12

Guide Words

The two words at the top of a dictionary page are called guide words. The first guide word is the same as the first word listed on the page. The second guide word is the same as the last word listed on the page. To find a word in the dictionary, decide if it comes in alphabetical order between the guide words on a page. If it does, you will find the word on that page.

Read each pair of guide words and the words that are listed below them. Circle the four words in each list that could be found on a page that has those guide words.

draw / foil	melt / pony	boat / cone
dime	past	crown
(drink)	open	bride
(face)	match	cloud
from	prize	call
(dust)	must	chain
(fire)	nine	cut

get / heavy	rose / stand	two / wrote
grow	rich	tractor
happy	slide	turtle
house	rush	under
icy	scarf	voice
give	some	world
goat	return	wind

ANTONYMS

Read the words below. In each row, circle the word that is an antonym (opposite) for the first word.

1. hard   deep   (soft)   free
2. sink   float   trap   run
3. right   less   hurt   wrong
4. after   first   before   near
5. fast   slow   many   pretty

Read each sentence and the words beside it. Circle, then write the word that is an antonym (opposite) for the word shown below each blank.

1. Turn a light __on__ so we can see.   around / (on)
   (off)

2. The _____ runner will win this race.   fastest / oldest
   (slowest)

3. The books are on a shelf _____ my head.   above / near
   (below)

4. The little boy has a _____ dog.   quiet / small
   (large)

ANTONYMS

Name _____

Read the list of words below. Then read the words that follow. Write an antonym (opposite) from the list for each word.

in	no	slow	bad	found	near
cry	stop	on	big	small	more
	night	last	cold	dry	

1. fast — slow
2. good — _____
3. out — _____
4. large — _____
5. start — _____
6. yes — _____
7. far — _____
8. day — _____
9. less — _____
10. hot — _____
11. laugh — _____
12. first — _____
13. lost — _____
14. off — _____
15. wet — _____
16. little — _____

 NAME _____

SYNONYMS

A synonym is a word that has the same or nearly the same meaning as another word.

small—little
sleep—nap
fast—quick

Read the words in each box. Draw a line to match each word with its synonym (word that has the same meaning).

shout	chilly		start	begin
big	large		sleep	look
cool	yell		see	rest

look	dad		under	city
pile	see		town	clean
father	stack		wash	below

sack	small		happy	road
little	bag		friend	pal
land	ground		street	glad

lift	speak		steps	close
talk	noisy		penny	stairs
loud	raise		shut	cent

SYNONYMS

Read the words below. In each row, circle the word that is a synonym (word that has the same meaning) for the first word.

1. friends   (pals)   boys   caps
2. bag   stand   sack   paper
3. big   new   free   large
4. sniff   smell   pet   nose
5. cool   good   chilly   high

Read each sentence and the words beside it. Circle, then write the word that is a synonym (word that has the same meaning) for the word shown below each blank.

1. Jodi's home is ____near____ mine.   like (near)
                    (close to)

2. I made a _____ trip to the store.   quick third
               (fast)

3. Dominic has a _____ on his face.   mark   smile
                    (grin)

4. We need to _____ our dog.   wash   find
                 (clean)

17

SYNONYMS

Read the list of words below. Then read the words that follow. Write a synonym (word that has the same meaning) from the list for each word.

fix   small   swift   song   supper   fire
cent   rock   near   throw   afraid   sniff
noisy   grin   rest   brook

1. mend _fix_
2. smell _____
3. tune _____
4. smile _____
5. dinner _____
6. sleep _____
7. fast _____
8. close _____

9. penny _____
10. pitch _____
11. stone _____
12. scared _____
13. stream _____
14. flame _____
15. tiny _____
16. loud _____

HOMOPHONES

Homophones are words that sound the same but have different spellings and different meanings.

sea—see
to—two
right—write

Read the words in each box. Draw a line to match each word on the left with a word on the right that is pronounced the same.

meat	made
maid	sail
sale	meet

weak	road
here	week
rode	hear

flower	deer
to	flour
dear	two

pane	plain
pail	pale
plane	pain

right	waste
would	write
waist	wood

bare	be
buy	bear
bee	by

sent	sea
eye	cent
see	I

knot	knight
night	not
new	knew

19

HOMOPHONES

Read the list of words below. Then read the words that follow. For each word write a word that is pronounced the same but spelled differently.

meat, here, waist, be, cent, two, deer
made, right, eye, knew, blue, sale, week

1. dear — deer
2. meet — meat
3. waste — waist
4. sail — sale
5. to — two
6. blew — blue
7. write — right
8. maid — made
9. weak — week
10. hear — here
11. bee — be
12. sent — cent
13. new — knew
14. I — eye

HOMOPHONES

Read the words below. In each row, circle the word that is pronounced the same as the first word.

1. here — (hear) — head — heel
2. cent — seed — sent — see
3. week — weak — weed — weep
4. sale — sail — safe — sat
5. road — robe — roast — rode

Read each sentence and the words beside it. Circle, then write the word that is pronounced the same as the word shown below each blank.

1. Jill ___blew___ dust off the old book.   (blew) beat
   (blue)

2. We saw ___two___ skunks in the woods.   ten (two)
   (too)

3. There is a bug in my ___eye___.   (eye) ear
   (I)

4. Julie will ___write___ a story in class.   (write) read
   (right)

5. I ___would___ like you to come to my party.   (would) waist
   (wood)

21

NAME

REVIEW

Read the words in each box. Draw a line to match each word with its antonym (opposite).

wrong	last	slow	happy
before	right	sad	hot
first	dark	weak	fast
light	after	cold	strong

Read the words in each box. Draw a line to match each word with its synonym (word that has the same meaning).

smell	clean	small	close
wash	grin	talk	steps
smile	sick	stairs	little
ill	sniff	shut	speak

Read the words in each box. Draw a line to match each word with its homophone (word that is pronounced the same).

meet	road	deer	right
rode	sale	write	I
two	meat	eye	by
sail	too	buy	dear

PROGRESS CHECK

Read the questions below. Answer each question by circling two words.

1. Which two words are antonyms?
   (cold)   small   (hot)   water

2. Which two words are synonyms?
   ill   well   glad   sick

3. Which two words are homophones?
   spend   sent   cent   penny

4. Which two words are antonyms?
   (fast)   near   (slow)   race

5. Which two words are synonyms?
   big   (large)   (small)   (size)

Read each pair of words below. Write **a** between each pair of antonyms. Write **s** between each pair of synonyms. Write **h** between words that are pronounced the same.

1. big __s__ large
2. dark _____ light
3. sail _____ sale
4. first _____ last

5. dear _____ deer
6. happy _____ sad
7. smile _____ grin
8. blue _____ blew

9. soft _____ hard
10. fast _____ quick
11. knew _____ new
12. lift _____ raise

23

Name _____

Endings: -ed and -ing

When a word ends with one vowel followed by a consonant, double the consonant before adding **-ed** or **-ing**.

hop
hopp**ed**
hopp**ing**

Read each sentence and the word beside it. Add **-ed** or **-ing** to the word to complete the sentence. Write the word in the blank.

1. I _____batted_____ the ball. bat

2. Who is _____ next to you in class? sit

3. I was _____ to catch the bus. run

4. Alec _____ the cat on its head. pat

5. Teri _____ the fence at our school. paint

6. Kevin is _____ Justin. help

24

Endings: -ed and -ing

When a word ends with **e**, drop the **e** before adding **-ed** or **-ing**.

smile
smil**ed**
smil**ing**

Read each sentence and the word beside it. Add **-ed** or **-ing** to the word to complete the sentence. Write the word in the blank.

1. Tony _____baked_____ a good loaf of bread. bake

2. I will be _____ my room soon. clean

3. Karla enjoys _____ to her friends. write

4. Mike _____ a good meal for us. cook

5. Sharon _____ the ball ten times. bounce

6. Diane is _____ the leaves now. rake

25

Endings: -ed and -ing

| When a word ends in a consonant followed by **y**, change the **y** to **i** before adding **-ed**. When a word ends in a vowel followed by **y**, just add **-ed**. Do not change **y** before adding **-ing** to a word that ends in **y**. | fry   fr**ied**
play play**ed**
fry   fry**ing** |

Read each sentence and the word beside it. Add **-ed** or **-ing** to the word to complete the sentence. Write the word in the blank.

1. Bob washed and _____dried_____ the dishes.   dry

2. My sister is _____ for a new job.   look

3. James _____ to get his work done.   hurry

4. Jared is _____ the books for us.   carry

5. We _____ your party very much.   enjoy

6. Caitlin is _____ a new dress.   buy

Base Words and Endings

A word to which an ending is added is called a base word. Read the list of words and base words in the box at the right.

Word	Base Word
popping	pop
smiling	smile
carried	carry

Read each word below. Then write its base word in the blank.

1. rubbed _rub_
2. crying _____
3. missed _____
4. smiled _____
5. taking _____
6. tried _____
7. stopped _____
8. clapping _____
9. played _____
10. tapped _____
11. writing _____
12. liked _____
13. carried _____
14. hummed _____

27

Name _____

Endings: -s and -es

Many words can be formed by adding -**s** to other words. When a word ends in **s**, **ss**, **sh**, **ch**, or **x**, add -**es**.

sings   catches
pass**es**   fix**es**
wash**es**

Read each word below. Add -**s** or -**es** to form a new word. Write the new word in the blank.

1. rush   rushes
2. miss   _____
3. help   _____
4. catch   _____
5. guess   _____
6. jump   _____
7. watch   _____

8. think   _____
9. reach   _____
10. work   _____
11. wax   _____
12. toss   _____
13. ask   _____
14. push   _____

Endings: -S and -ES

When a word ends with a consonant followed by **y**, change the **y** to **i** and add **-es**. When a word ends in a vowel followed by **y**, just add **-s**.

sit	sit**s**
cry	cri**es**
play	play**s**

Read each word below. Add **-s** or **-es** to form a new word. Write the new word in the blank.

1. try   tries
2. say
3. study
4. buy
5. fly
6. hurry
7. tray

8. marry
9. fry
10. lay
11. stay
12. copy
13. dry
14. enjoy

Endings: -s and -es

Read each sentence and the word beside it. Add **-s** or **-es** to the word to complete the sentence. Write the word in the blank.

1. LuAnn __carries__ her lunch to work. carry

2. My puppy _____ for bones. beg

3. Tela _____ her teeth after each meal. brush

4. Our team always _____ to play its best. try

5. Our club _____ toys for friends. fix

6. The bus _____ us to school. take

7. Our band _____ in big parades. march

8. Mrs. Smith _____ first grade. teach

NAME _____

ENDINGS: -ER AND -EST

| The ending **-er** sometimes means "more." For example, **smaller** means "more small." The ending **-est** means "most." For example, **smallest** means "most small." | small
small**er**
small**est** |

Look at the pictures and read the words. Draw a line from each word to the picture it tells about.

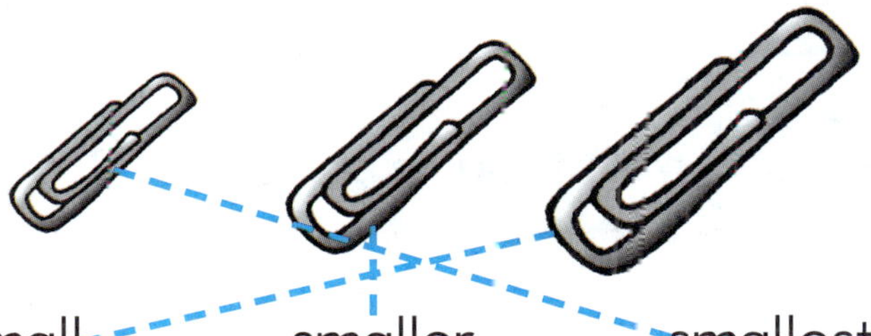

small — smaller — smallest

tall   taller   tallest

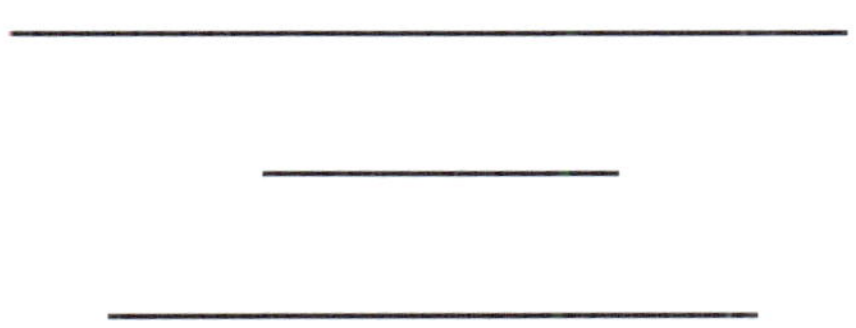

_____
_____
____

long   longer   longest

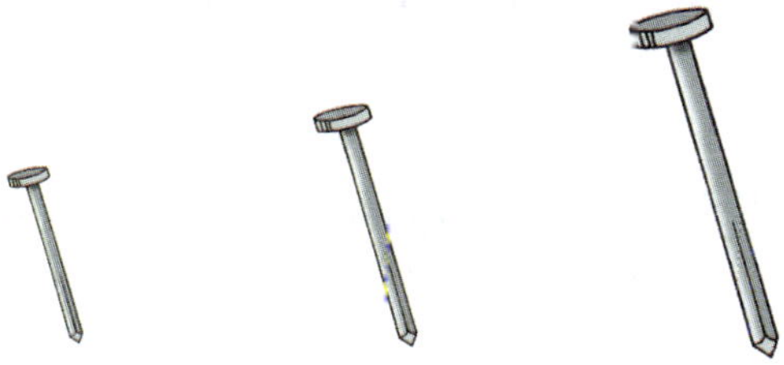

short   shorter   shortest

little   littler   littlest

large   larger   largest

31

Endings: -ER and -EST

The ending **-er** can be used to compare two things. The ending **-est** can be used to compare more than two things.

Read each sentence and the words beside it. Circle, then write the word that makes sense in each sentence.

1. The tree is ___taller___ than Buttons. tall (taller)

2. My cat is a _____ color than my dog. light lighter

3. That is the _____ tree in these woods. older oldest

4. My hair is _____ than yours. dark darker

5. The blue car is the _____ of all. smaller smallest

6. Tom's turtle was _____ than mine. slow slower

7. Sam is the _____ boy in the class. faster fastest

32

Endings: -ER and -EST

Read each sentence and the word beside it. Add **-er** or **-est** to the word to complete the sentence. Write the word in the blank.

1. Buttons is ____slower____ than Mindy. slow

2. This plant is the _____ in my garden. tall

3. I will take _____ walks than before. long

4. Drake's pillow is _____ than mine. soft

5. Play the _____ note in this song. high

6. This test is the _____ one of all. hard

7. Dawn's shirt looks _____ than mine. clean

8. The river is _____ than the stream. wide

NAME

REVIEW

Read each word below. Add the ending shown beside the word to form a new word. Write the new word in the blank.

1. wash + s or es = _washes_

2. carry + s = _____

3. dark + er = _____

4. smile + ing = _____

5. near + est = _____

6. stop + ing = _____

7. close + ed = _____

8. smart + est = _____

PROGRESS CHECK

Read each sentence and the word beside it. Add an ending from the list below to the word. Write the word in the blank. You may use an ending more than once.   -ed   -ing   -s   -es   -er   -est

1. Mom ___hurried___ to work this morning.   hurry

2. The puppy _____ the ball.   drop

3. This is the _____ hill in our town.   steep

4. A free pencil _____ with the paper.   come

5. Jim _____ the ball for our team.   catch

6. Marsha is _____ at me.   smile

7. Is your pen _____ than mine?   new

8. Anna will be _____ her nap soon.   take

35

PLURALS: -S AND -ES

You can make many words mean "more than one" by adding **-s** to base words. When a word ends in **s, ss, sh, ch,** or **x**, add **-es** to make it mean "more than one."

lids	wish**es**
bus**es**	patch**es**
dress**es**	fox**es**

Read the list of words below. Then look at the pictures. Add **-s** or **-es** to a word from the list to name the pictures in each box. Write the word in the blank.

| watch | rake | bird | ax | hand |
| glass | bus | duck | mop | peach |

birds

_____

_____

_____

_____

_____

_____

_____

_____

_____

Plurals: -s and -es

When a word ends in a consonant followed by **y**, change the **y** to **i** and add **-es** to make it mean "more than one." When a word ends in a vowel followed by **y**, just add **-s**.

tray	tray**s**
story	stor**ies**
boy	boy**s**

Read the words below. Change each word to make it mean "more than one." Write the new word in the blank.

1. baby _babies_
2. key _____
3. pony _____
4. bunny _____
5. toy _____
6. watch _____
7. daisy _____
8. day _____
9. wish _____
10. book _____
11. fox _____
12. party _____
13. frog _____
14. penny _____

PLURALS: -S AND -ES

Read each sentence and the word beside it. Change the word to make it mean "more than one." Write the new word in the blank.

1. Bob put ten _____cans_____ of food on the shelf.   can

2. Erica likes sliced _____ with cream.   peach

3. Our class was standing in two _____.   line

4. The frogs like to eat _____.   fly

5. A big town can have many _____.   park

6. Sierra has two _____ in his hand.   penny

7. Two wild _____ ran into the woods.   fox

8. All three of those _____ sing well.   boy

38

Read each sentence and the words beside it. Circle the word that makes sense in the sentence and change it to make it mean "more than one." Write the word in the blank.

1. We stacked the ____dishes____ on a shelf.　　(dish) / door

2. Two _____ made a nest in the tree.　　bird / bike

3. I put six _____ into the bank.　　penny / party

4. Many _____ pass my home each day.　　bus / bag

5. We rested on _____ after the game.　　bench / bush

6. Hellen went to three birthday _____.　　party / pony

7. We use _____ for chopping wood.　　ax / ash

8. I had two _____ for my lunch.　　watch / peach

39

Progress Check

Read the words. Change each word to make it mean "more than one." Write the new word in the blank.

1. watch watches
2. bunny _____
3. game _____
4. city _____
5. wish _____
6. key _____
7. peach _____
8. penny _____
9. hand _____
10. cup _____
11. fly _____
12. fox _____
13. daisy _____
14. match _____
15. toy _____
16. box _____

Adding 's

To show that something belongs to a person or thing, add **'s** to the end of the word that names the owner.

girl's hat

Read each group of words below. Then add **'s** to the underlined word that names the owner. Write both underlined words in the blank.

1. the <u>robe</u> of <u>Dad</u>   *Dad's robe*

2. the <u>bone</u> of the <u>dog</u>

3. a <u>sled</u> that the <u>girl</u> has

4. the <u>cat</u> that <u>Ray</u> owns

5. the <u>thorn</u> of the <u>rose</u>

6. a <u>pen</u> that <u>Ann</u> has

7. the <u>sister</u> of <u>Pat</u>

8. the <u>smile</u> of the <u>boy</u>

Adding 's

Read each sentence and the words beside it. Circle, then write the word that makes sense in each sentence.

1. My _bike's_ tire has gone flat.   bike / (bike's)

2. The _____ walked to school.   girls / girl's

3. Her _____ hat fits just right.   dads / dad's

4. My _____ coat is just like mine.   friends / friend's

5. The _____ are closed.   bank's / banks

6. My _____ eyes are brown.   mothers / mother's

7. Those _____ have the same shirts.   boy's / boys

8. That _____ car is new.   man's / mans

42

Adding 's

Read each sentence and the words beside it. Add 's to one of the words so it makes sense in the sentence. Circle, then write the new word in the blank.

1. Did __Jane's__ cat run away?   (Jane) / Jump / Jam

2. I like to watch the _____ new chicks.   head / hen / help

3. The _____ cup is too full.   bone / bow / boy

4. The _____ pages are torn.   book / boot / boom

5. _____ home is on my street.   Took / Top / Tom

6. Is the _____ water dish blue?   door / dot / dog

7. I will hang _____ coat on a hook.   Bill / Bike / Big

8. Our _____ cage is clean.   bone / bird / book

43

NAME _____

REVIEW

Read each group of words below. Then add 's to the underlined word that names the owner. Write both underlined words in the blank.

1. the <u>tail</u> of the <u>kite</u> — kite's tail

2. the <u>hat</u> that <u>Dan</u> has

3. the <u>paw</u> of the <u>cat</u>

4. a <u>book</u> that <u>Mom</u> owns

5. the <u>leg</u> of the <u>chair</u>

6. a <u>bike</u> that <u>Ben</u> has

7. the <u>flute</u> of <u>Amy</u>

8. the <u>game</u> of the <u>girl</u>

9. the <u>arm</u> of the <u>boy</u>

PROGRESS CHECK

Read each sentence and the words beside it. Add 's to one of the words so it makes sense in the sentence. Circle, then write the new word in the blank.

1. Our ____town's____ stores are big. — too / tune / (town)

2. This _____ counter is full of toys. — stop / shop / spot

3. The _____ color is dark red. — ash / apple / at

4. My _____ painting is pretty. — fatter / father / feather

5. That _____ head is huge. — lion / lean / leaf

6. The _____ ears are long and floppy. — dot / dog / dig

7. _____ coat is the same color as mine. — Jump / Jill / Jeep

8. The _____ leaves are falling. — trap / tree / trot

45

Name

Compound Words

A compound word is formed by joining two smaller words together.

tea + pot = teapot

Read each compound word below. Write the two words that form each compound word.

1. baseball — base — ball

2. doghouse — ____ — ____

3. snowflake — ____ — ____

4. flashlight — ____ — ____

5. popcorn — ____ — ____

6. raincoat — ____ — ____

7. bathtub — ____ — ____

8. sailboat — ____ — ____

Compound Words

Read the words in each list. Draw lines to show words that form compound words.

row	ship
bath	tub
mail	boat
rain	box
space	print
gold	fish
foot	coat

Read the sentences below. Write a compound word from the exercise above to complete each sentence.

1. A __rowboat__ was on the lake.

2. Shawn filled the _____ with water.

3. A _____ took off for the moon.

4. Wayne put a letter in the _____.

5. Each step left my _____ in the sand.

6. A big _____ swims in the pond.

7. Anthony wore his yellow _____.

Compound Words

Read each sentence below. Use two words from the sentence to form a compound word. Write the word in the blank.

1. A bird that is blue is a ___bluebird___.

2. A burn from the sun is a _____.

3. A drop of rain is a _____.

4. The end of a week is a _____.

5. A boat with a sail is a _____.

6. A room where a class meets is a _____.

7. A pole where a flag flies is a _____.

8. A ball you kick with your foot is a _____.

48

NAME _____

Review

Read each sentence below. Use two words from the sentence to form a compound word. Write the word in the blank.

1. A coat worn in the rain is a __raincoat__.

2. The print your foot makes is a _____.

3. A shell from the sea is a _____.

4. A paper that tells news is a _____.

5. A fish that is gold is a _____.

6. The day of your birth is your _____.

7. A plane that flies in the air is an _____.

8. A box that holds sand is a _____.

49

Progress Check

Read the words in each list. Then read the sentences that follow. Choose a word from list **A** and a word from list **B** to form a compound word that completes each sentence. Write the word in the blank.

A	B
rain	noon
base	house
flash	end
after	light
dog	storm
pop	corn
week	ball

1. Last night's __rainstorm__ soaked the garden.

2. Runt ran into his _____.

3. My _____ let us see the best path.

4. Two classes will play a game of _____.

5. Our class reads in the _____.

6. The _____ tastes good.

7. I will see you at the game next _____.

CONTRACTIONS

NAME _____

A contraction is a short way to write two words. It is written by putting two words together and leaving out a letter or letters. An apostrophe takes the place of the letter or letters that are left out. The word **won't** is a special contraction made from the words **will** and **not**.

is + not = **isn't**
I + am = **I'm**
let + us = **let's**
will + not = **won't**

Read the list of words below. Then read the word pairs that follow. Write a contraction from the list for each word pair.

| hasn't | can't | let's | isn't | won't | haven't |
| weren't | I'm | aren't | wasn't | didn't | doesn't |

1. have not haven't
2. was not _____
3. let us _____
4. will not _____
5. does not _____
6. has not _____

7. are not _____
8. is not _____
9. did not _____
10. can not _____
11. I am _____
12. were not _____

51

CONTRACTIONS

Read each contraction below. Then write the two words for which each contraction stands.

I + will = I'll
we + are = we're

1. she'll — she will
2. they're
3. we'll
4. he'll
5. you're
6. I'll
7. we're
8. they'll
9. you'll

CONTRACTIONS

Read each sentence below. Write the contraction for the words shown under the blank in each sentence.

I + have = **I've**
it + is = **it's**

1. Meghan said __she's__ your friend.
   (she is)

2. Baine thinks _____ going to the show.
   (he is)

3. It seems _____ studied for a long time.
   (you have)

4. _____ been playing baseball today.
   (They have)

5. _____ easy to write my name.
   (It is)

6. _____ been reading a good book.
   (I have)

7. _____ been gone a long time.
   (We have)

8. _____ been sick for three days.
   (You have)

53

Review

Read each sentence below. Write the contraction for the words shown below the blank in each sentence.

1. Ashley _____won't_____ be late for school.
   (will not)

2. Vickie and Bob said _____ see us later.
   (they will)

3. Fran says _____ going to her friend's house.
   (she is)

4. _____ need a rest stop after the long hike.
   (We will)

5. You _____ swim by yourself.
   (should not)

6. _____ going to see snow falling soon.
   (We are)

7. The blue swimsuit _____ my first choice.
   (was not)

8. _____ glad to see you.
   (I am)

Progress Check

Read each pair of words below. Write the contraction for each word pair.

1. did not   didn't
2. she is
3. he will
4. I have
5. you will
6. they are
7. she will
8. has not
9. we are
10. it is
11. let us
12. I am
13. will not
14. is not
15. are not
16. you are

NAME _____

PREFIXES

A prefix is a letter or group of letters that can be added to the beginning of a word. The prefix **re-** means "again." For example, the word **refill** means "fill again."

re + fill = **re**fill

Read each word below. Add the prefix **re-** to form a new word. Write the new word in the blank.

1. make remake
2. paint _____
3. do _____
4. play _____

Read each sentence and the words beside it. Circle, then write the word that makes sense in each sentence.

1. We will replant our garden.   repaint / (replant)

2. Please _____ the story.   refold / reread

3. Logan will _____ the cold meat.   rewrite / reheat

4. Kathleen will _____ the glass.   retell / refill

NAME

PREFIXES

| The prefix **un-** means "not" or "the opposite of." For example, the word **unlock** means "the opposite of lock." | un + lock = unlock |

Read each word below. Add the prefix **un-** to form a new word. Write the new word in the blank.

1. fair   _unfair_
2. wrap   _____
3. happy _____
4. pack   _____

Read each sentence and the words beside it. Circle, then write the word that makes sense in each sentence.

1. Will you help me _untie_ this knot?   undress / (untie)

2. The little girl looked _____.   unhappy / unlocked

3. Did Andrew _____ his gift yet?   unwrap / unfair

4. Mom will _____ the box of dishes.   unsafe / unpack

57

PREFIXES

Read each sentence and the word beside it. Add **re-** or **un-** to the word to complete each sentence. The word you form must make sense in the sentence.

1. I must _reread_ this book. read

2. Was Paul _____ to you? kind

3. I will _____ this story. tell

4. Can you _____ the picture? draw

5. Jeremy must _____ his work. write

6. The new rule of the game is _____. fair

7. It is _____ to throw away your paper. wise

8. Driving too fast is _____. safe

SUFFIXES

A suffix is a letter or group of letters that can be added to the end of a word. The suffix -**ful** usually means "full of." For example, the word helpful means "full of help."

play + **ful** = play**ful**

Read each word below. Add the suffix -**ful** to form a new word. Write the new word in the blank.

1. color colorful
2. care _____
3. use _____
4. pain _____

Read each sentence and the words beside it. Circle, then write the word that makes sense in each sentence.

1. I was thankful to get home.   useful / (thankful)

2. The falling leaves are very _____.   colorful / careful

3. My cut hand is _____.   playful / painful

4. I have a _____ smile on my face.   joyful / useful

59

Suffixes

The suffix **-ly** can be added to some words. For example, something done in a **nice** way is done **nicely**.

nice + ly = nicely

Read each word below. Add the suffix **-ly** to form a new word. Write the new word in the blank.

1. soft _softly_
2. friend _____
3. slow _____
4. brave _____

Read each sentence and the words beside it. Circle, then write the word that makes sense in each sentence.

1. Dress _warmly_ when it is cold. — (warmly) / badly

2. The gloves fit too _____. — tightly / slowly

3. The little girl pet the kitten _____. — softly / nearly

4. Buddy ran _____ down the street. — quickly / fairly

Suffixes

Read each sentence and the word beside it. Add **-ful** or **-ly** to the word to complete each sentence. The word you form must make sense in the sentence.

1. I am __hopeful__ of winning the prize.   hope

2. Be sure to write your name _____.   neat

3. Be _____ when you cross the street.   care

4. Dan plays the horn _____.   loud

5. Joshua _____ gave up his turn.   glad

6. Our new puppy is very _____.   play

7. I like your _____ smile.   friend

8. We study many _____ things in school.   use

61

Review

Read the list of prefixes and suffixes below. Then add one of the prefixes or suffixes to the underlined word in each group of words. Write the new word in the blank.

re-   un-   -ful   -ly

1. to <u>fill</u> again — refill

2. the opposite of <u>happy</u>

3. in a <u>quick</u> way

4. full of <u>hope</u>

5. full of <u>pain</u>

6. in a <u>safe</u> way

7. the opposite of <u>fair</u>

8. to <u>read</u> again

Syllables

Many words are made of small parts called syllables. Because each syllable has one vowel sound, a word has as many syllables as it has vowel sounds. The word **stone** has one vowel sound, so it has one syllable. The word **raincoat** has two vowel sounds, so it has two syllables.

Name the pictures. Write the number of syllables you hear in each picture name.

bathtub _2_	umbrella _____	slipper _____
chick _____	fork _____	pocket _____
bird _____	garden _____	butterfly _____
valentine _____	frog _____	wagon _____

NAME _____

PROGRESS CHECK

Read the words below. Write each word and draw a line between its syllables.

1. airplane — air/plane
2. lightly
3. useful
4. refill
5. unfair
6. glassful
7. raindrop
8. rewrap
9. lately
10. undress

ANSWER KEY

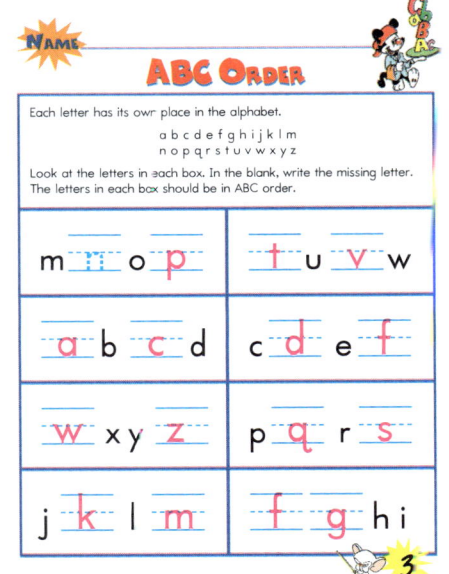
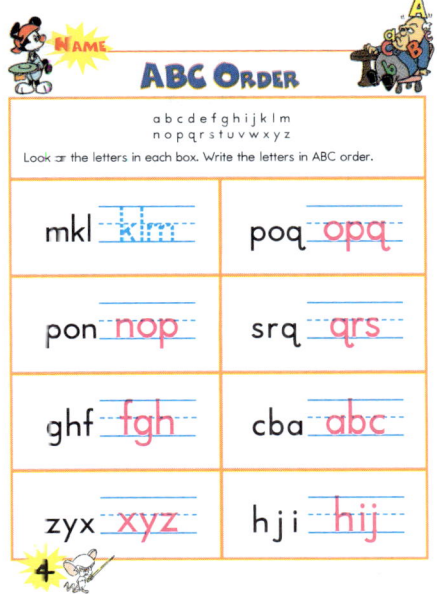

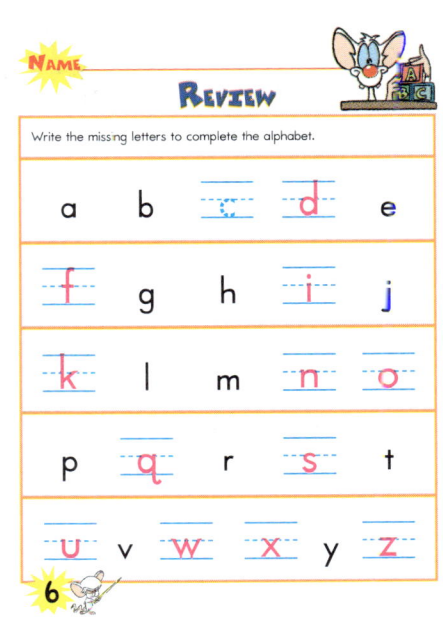

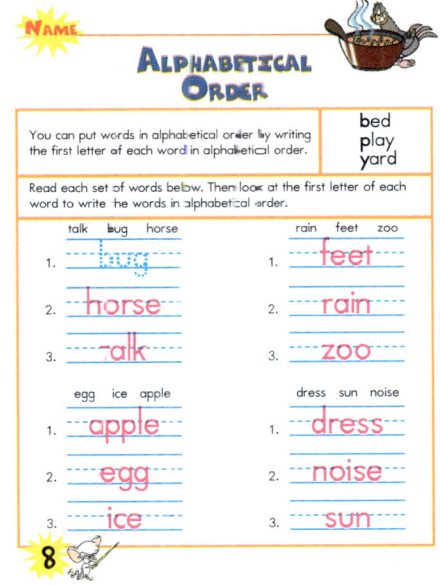

65

Answer Key

Page 9 — Alphabetical Order

Read each set of words below. Then look at the first letter of each word to write the words in alphabetical order.

like work down
1. down
2. like
3. work

jump can stop
1. can
2. jump
3. stop

wet miss fun ant
1. ant
2. fun
3. miss
4. wet

yard hen bag ox
1. bag
2. hen
3. ox
4. yard

Page 10 — Alphabetical Order

When words begin with the same letter, use the second letters to put the words in alphabetical order.

dog
dish
draw

Read each set of words below. Write the words in alphabetical order.

ax ask and
1. and
2. ask
3. ax

give gas get
1. gas
2. get
3. give

sun sack song
1. sack
2. song
3. sun

east eye egg
1. east
2. egg
3. eye

Page 11 — Review

Read each set of words below. Then write the words in alphabetical order. You may have to look at the second letter in some words.

truck lock gate
1. gate
2. lock
3. truck

bake brake blue
1. bake
2. blue
3. brake

stay scrub shell slip
1. scrub
2. shell
3. slip
4. stay

up pass know cow
1. cow
2. know
3. pass
4. up

Page 12 — Progress Check

Read each set of words below. Then look at the first or second letter of each word to write the words in alphabetical order.

crab car clock
1. car
2. clock
3. crab

wash ring need
1. need
2. ring
3. wash

pet bird duck cat
1. bird
2. cat
3. duck
4. pet

old one off open
1. off
2. old
3. one
4. open

Page 13 — Guide Words

The two words at the top of a dictionary page are called guide words. The first guide word is the same as the first word listed on the page. The second guide word is the same as the last word listed on the page. To find a word in the dictionary, decide if it comes in alphabetical order between the guide words on a page. If it does, you will find the word on that page.

Read each pair of guide words and the words that are listed below them. Circle the four words in each list that could be found on a page that has those guide words.

draw / foil
dime
(drink)
(face)
from
(dust)
(fire)

melt / pony
(past)
(open)
match
prize
(must)
(nine)

boat / cone
crown
(bride)
(cloud)
(call)
(chain)
cut

get / heavy
(grow)
(happy)
house
icy
(give)
(goat)

rose / stand
rich
(slide)
(rush)
(scarf)
(some)
return

two / wrote
tractor
turtle
(under)
(voice)
world
(wind)

Page 14 — Antonyms

Read the words below. In each row, circle the word that is an antonym (opposite) for the first word.

1. hard — deep — (soft) — free
2. sink — (float) — trap — run
3. right — less — hurt — (wrong)
4. after — first — (before) — near
5. fast — (slow) — many — pretty

Read each sentence and the words beside it. Circle, then write the word that is an antonym (opposite) for the word shown below each blank.

1. Turn a light __on__ so we can see. (off)   around (on)
2. The __fastest__ runner will win this race. (slowest)   (fastest) oldest
3. The books are on a shelf __above__ my head. (below)   (above) near
4. The little boy has a __small__ dog. (large)   quiet (small)

Answer Key

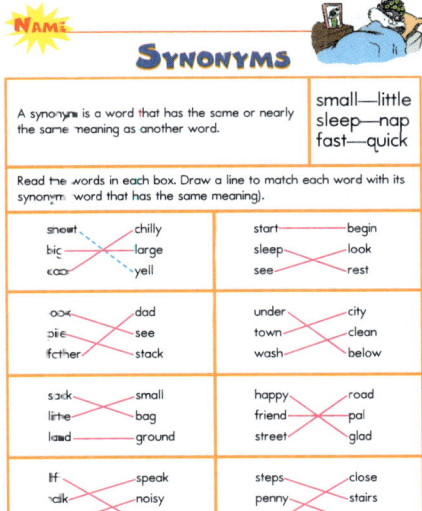
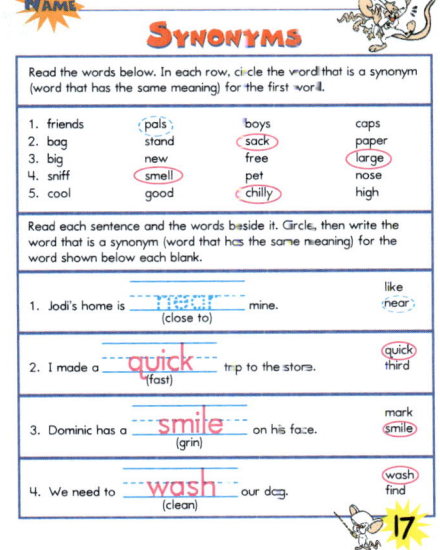
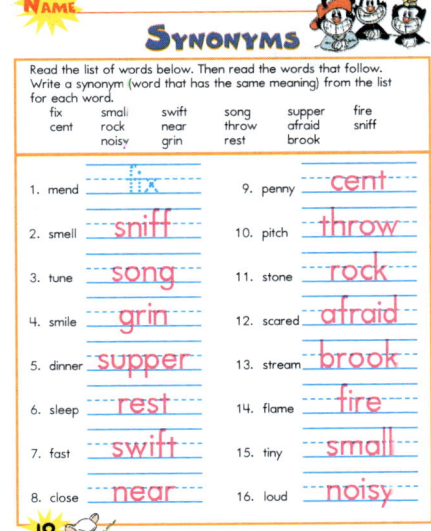
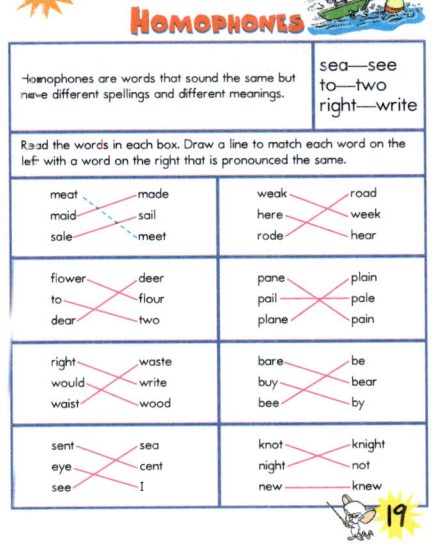
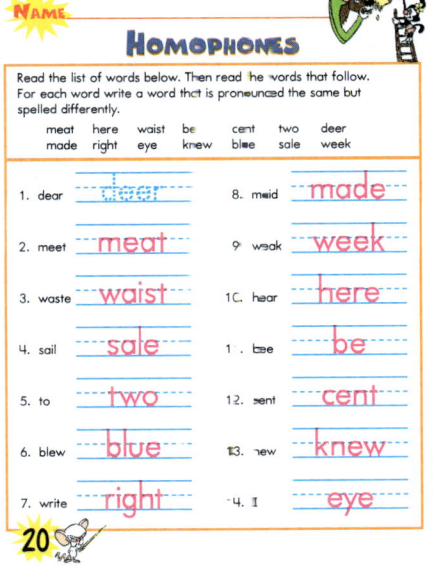

Answer Key

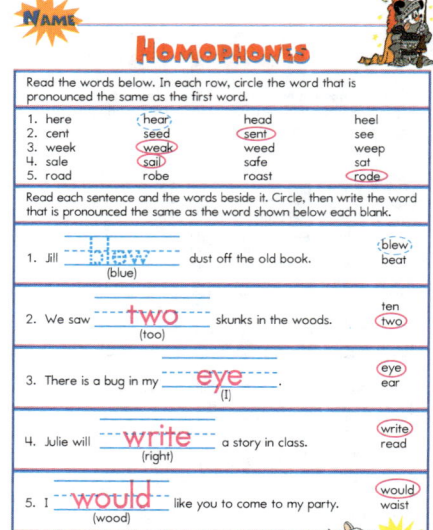

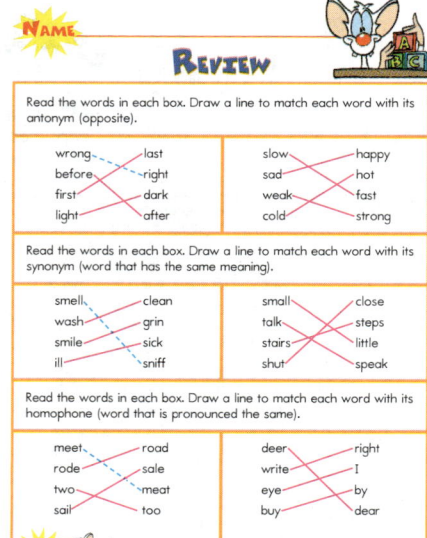

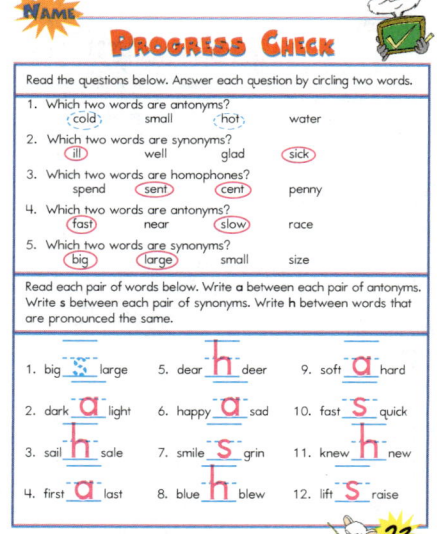

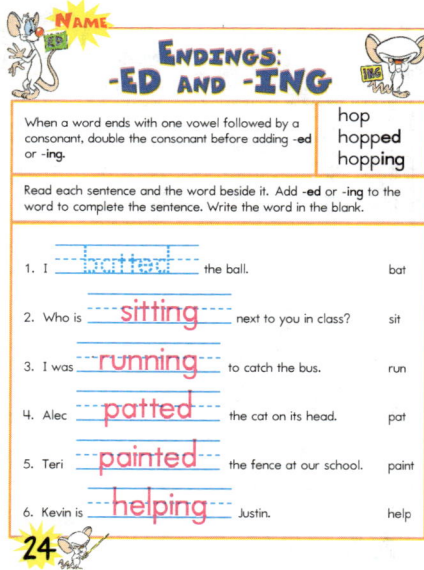

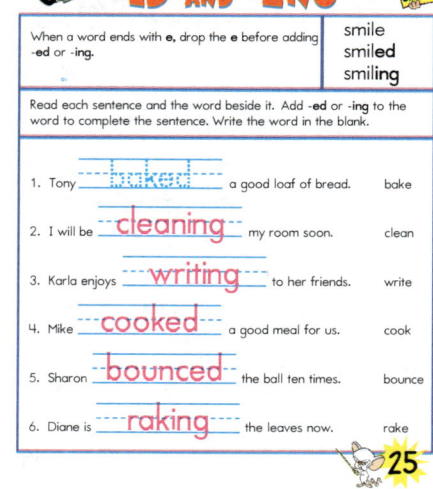

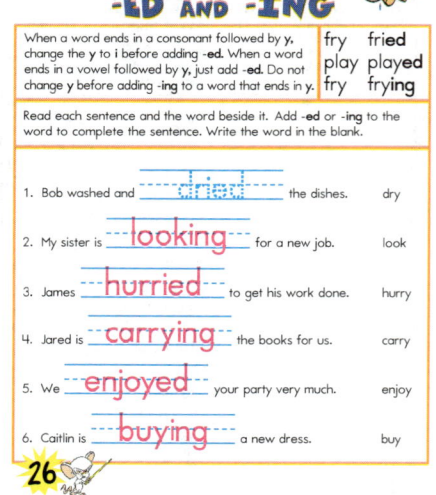

ANSWER KEY

Base Words and Endings (p. 27)

A word to which an ending is added is called a base word. Read the list of words and base words in the box at the right.

Word	Base Word
popping	pop
smiling	smile
carried	carry

Read each word below. Then write its base word in the blank.

1. rubbed — rub
2. crying — cry
3. missed — miss
4. smiled — smile
5. taking — take
6. tried — try
7. stopped — stop
8. clapping — clap
9. played — play
10. tapped — tap
11. writing — write
12. liked — like
13. carried — carry
14. hummed — hum

Endings: -s and -es (p. 28)

Many words can be formed by adding -s to other words. When a word ends in s, ss, sh, ch, or x, add -es.

sings, catches, passes, fixes, washes

Read each word below. Add -s or -es to form a new word. Write the new word in the blank.

1. rush — rushes
2. miss — misses
3. help — helps
4. catch — catches
5. guess — guesses
6. jump — jumps
7. watch — watches
8. think — thinks
9. reach — reaches
10. work — works
11. wax — waxes
12. toss — tosses
13. ask — asks
14. push — pushes

Endings: -s and -es (p. 29)

When a word ends with a consonant followed by y, change the y to i and add -es. When a word ends in a vowel followed by y, just add -s.

sit sits, cry cries, play plays

Read each word below. Add -s or -es to form a new word. Write the new word in the blank.

1. try — tries
2. say — says
3. study — studies
4. buy — buys
5. fly — flies
6. hurry — hurries
7. tray — trays
8. marry — marries
9. fry — fries
10. lay — lays
11. stay — stays
12. copy — copies
13. dry — dries
14. enjoy — enjoys

Endings: -s and -es (p. 30)

Read each sentence and the word beside it. Add -s or -es to the word to complete the sentence. Write the word in the blank.

1. LuAnn **carries** her lunch to work. (carry)
2. My puppy **begs** for bones. (beg)
3. Tela **brushes** her teeth after each meal. (brush)
4. Our team always **tries** to play its best. (try)
5. Our club **fixes** toys for friends. (fix)
6. The bus **takes** us to school. (take)
7. Our band **marches** in big parades. (march)
8. Mrs. Smith **teaches** first grade. (teach)

Endings: -er and -est (p. 31)

The ending -er sometimes means "more." For example, smaller means "more small." The ending -est means "most." For example, smallest means "most small."

small, smaller, smallest

Look at the pictures and read the words. Draw a line from each word to the picture it tells about.

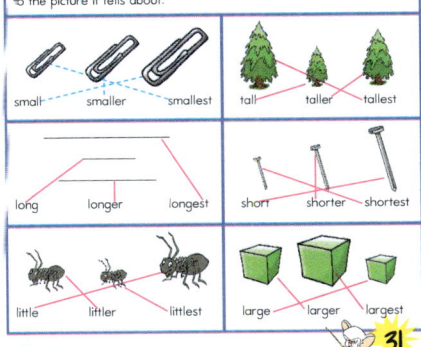

small — smaller — smallest; tall — taller — tallest; long — longer — longest; short — shorter — shortest; little — littler — littlest; large — larger — largest

Endings: -er and -est (p. 32)

The ending -er can be used to compare two things. The ending -est can be used to compare more than two things.

Read each sentence and the words beside it. Circle, then write the word that makes sense in each sentence.

1. The tree is **taller** than Buttons. (taller)
2. My cat is a **lighter** color than my dog. (lighter)
3. That is the **oldest** tree in these woods. (oldest)
4. My hair is **darker** than yours. (darker)
5. The blue car is the **smallest** of all. (smallest)
6. Tom's turtle was **slower** than mine. (slower)
7. Sam is the **fastest** boy in the class. (fastest)

69

Answer Key

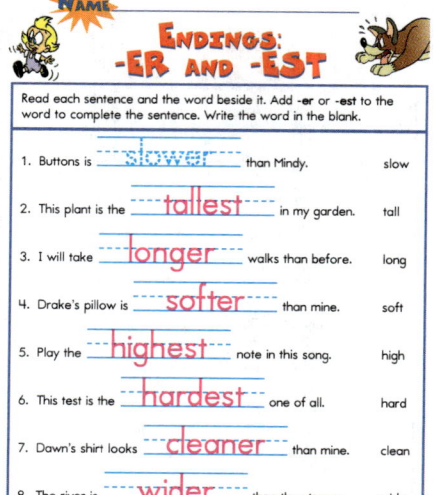

Endings: -ER and -EST

Read each sentence and the word beside it. Add -er or -est to the word to complete the sentence. Write the word in the blank.

1. Buttons is **slower** than Mindy. — slow
2. This plant is the **tallest** in my garden. — tall
3. I will take **longer** walks than before. — long
4. Drake's pillow is **softer** than mine. — soft
5. Play the **highest** note in this song. — high
6. This test is the **hardest** one of all. — hard
7. Dawn's shirt looks **cleaner** than mine. — clean
8. The river is **wider** than the stream. — wide

33

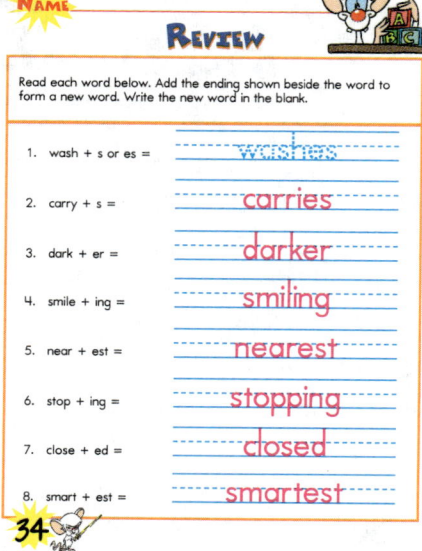

Review

Read each word below. Add the ending shown beside the word to form a new word. Write the new word in the blank.

1. wash + s or es = **washes**
2. carry + s = **carries**
3. dark + er = **darker**
4. smile + ing = **smiling**
5. near + est = **nearest**
6. stop + ing = **stopping**
7. close + ed = **closed**
8. smart + est = **smartest**

34

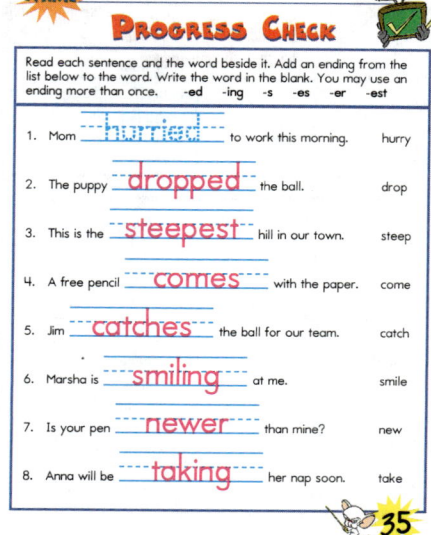

Progress Check

Read each sentence and the word beside it. Add an ending from the list below to the word. Write the word in the blank. You may use an ending more than once. -ed -ing -s -es -er -est

1. Mom **hurried** to work this morning. — hurry
2. The puppy **dropped** the ball. — drop
3. This is the **steepest** hill in our town. — steep
4. A free pencil **comes** with the paper. — come
5. Jim **catches** the ball for our team. — catch
6. Marsha is **smiling** at me. — smile
7. Is your pen **newer** than mine? — new
8. Anna will be **taking** her nap soon. — take

35

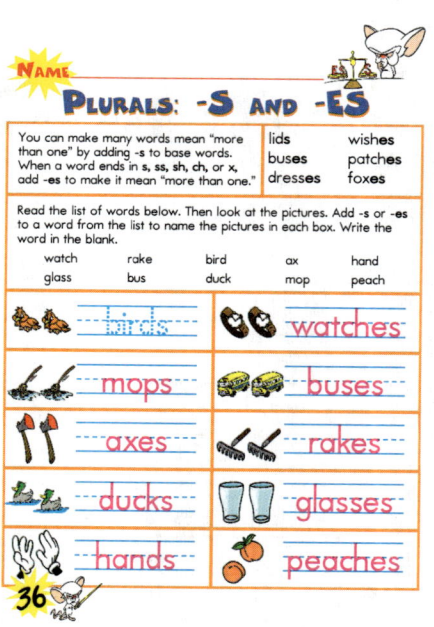

Plurals: -S and -ES

You can make many words mean "more than one" by adding -s to base words. When a word ends in s, ss, sh, ch, or x, add -es to make it mean "more than one."

lids wishes
buses patches
dresses foxes

Read the list of words below. Then look at the pictures. Add -s or -es to a word from the list to name the pictures in each box. Write the word in the blank.

watch rake bird ax hand
glass bus duck mop peach

birds	**watches**
mops	**buses**
axes	**rakes**
ducks	**glasses**
hands	**peaches**

36

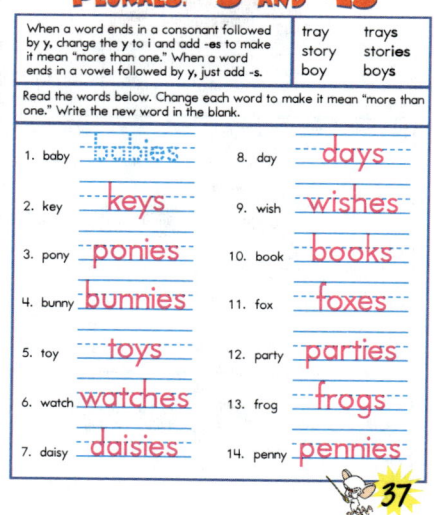

Plurals: -S and -ES

When a word ends in a consonant followed by y, change the y to i and add -es to make it mean "more than one." When a word ends in a vowel followed by y, just add -s.

tray trays
story stories
boy boys

Read the words below. Change each word to make it mean "more than one." Write the new word in the blank.

1. baby **babies**
2. key **keys**
3. pony **ponies**
4. bunny **bunnies**
5. toy **toys**
6. watch **watches**
7. daisy **daisies**
8. day **days**
9. wish **wishes**
10. book **books**
11. fox **foxes**
12. party **parties**
13. frog **frogs**
14. penny **pennies**

37

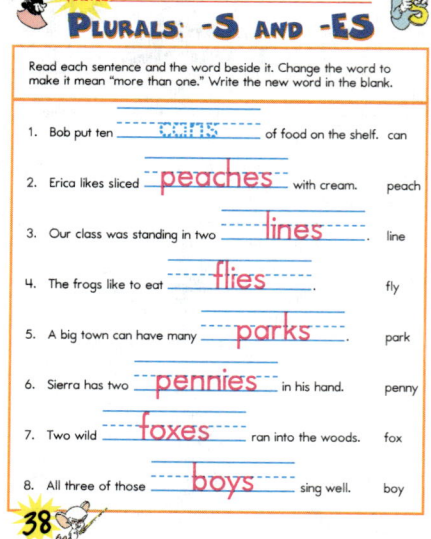

Plurals: -S and -ES

Read each sentence and the word beside it. Change the word to make it mean "more than one." Write the new word in the blank.

1. Bob put ten **cans** of food on the shelf. — can
2. Erica likes sliced **peaches** with cream. — peach
3. Our class was standing in two **lines**. — line
4. The frogs like to eat **flies**. — fly
5. A big town can have many **parks**. — park
6. Sierra has two **pennies** in his hand. — penny
7. Two wild **foxes** ran into the woods. — fox
8. All three of those **boys** sing well. — boy

38

ANSWER KEY

39 — Review
1. dishes
2. birds
3. pennies
4. buses
5. benches
6. parties
7. axes
8. peaches

Circled: dish, bird, penny, bus, bench, party, ax, peach

40 — Progress Check
1. watches
2. bunnies
3. games
4. cities
5. wishes
6. keys
7. peaches
8. pennies
9. hands
10. cups
11. flies
12. foxes
13. daisies
14. matches
15. toys
16. boxes

41 — Adding 's
1. Dad's robe
2. dog's bone
3. girl's sled
4. Ray's cat
5. rose's thorn
6. Ann's pen
7. Pat's sister
8. boy's smile

42 — Adding 's
1. bike's
2. girls
3. dad's
4. friend's
5. banks
6. mother's
7. boys
8. man's

Circled: bike's, girls, dad's, friend's, banks, mother's, boys, man's

43 — Adding 's
1. Jane's
2. hen's
3. boy's
4. book's
5. Tom's
6. dog's
7. Bill's
8. bird's

Circled: Jane, hen, boy, book, Tom, dog, Bill, bird

44 — Review
1. kite's tail
2. Dan's hat
3. cat's paw
4. Mom's book
5. chair's leg
6. Ben's bike
7. Amy's flute
8. girl's game
9. boy's arm

ANSWER KEY

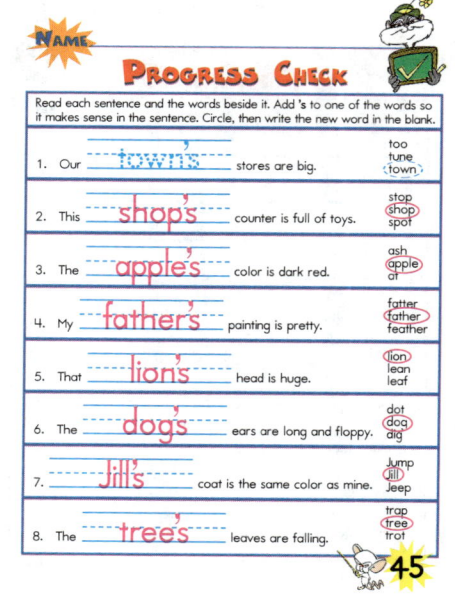
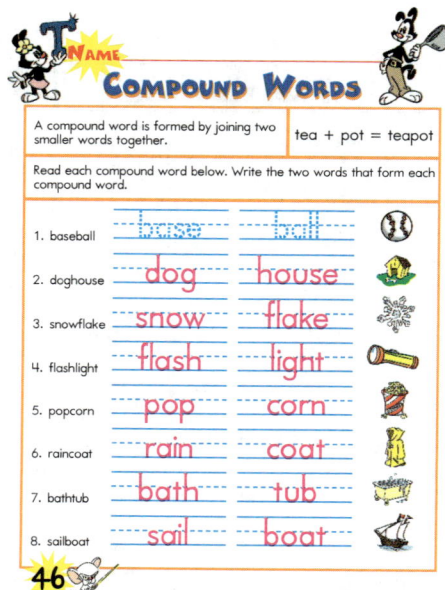
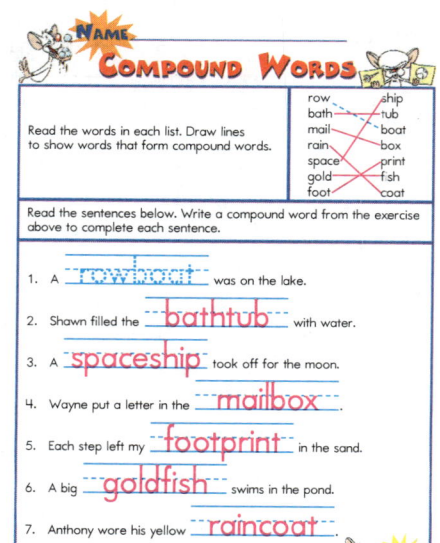
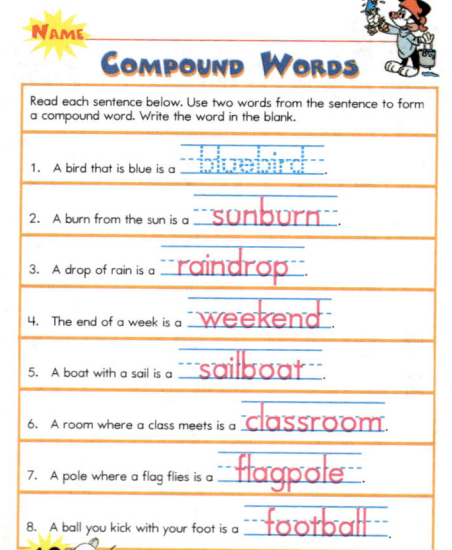
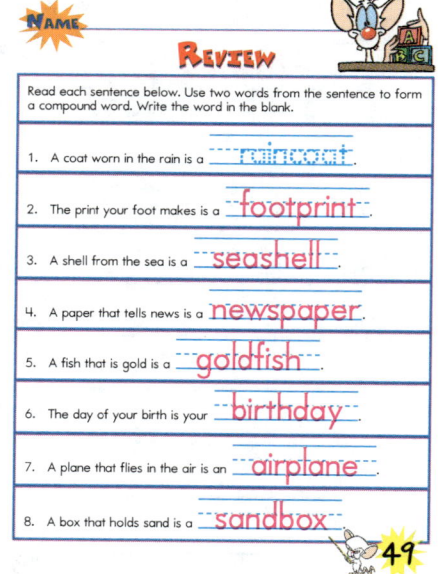
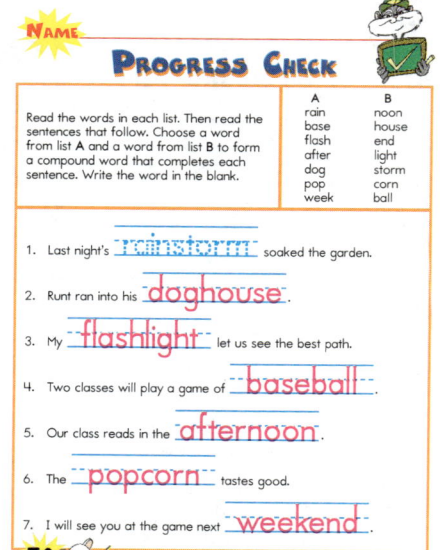

Answer Key

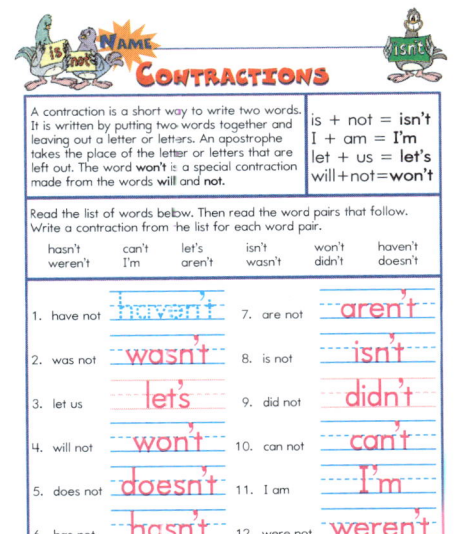
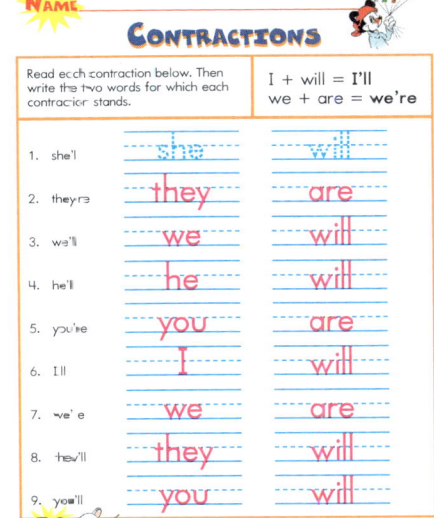
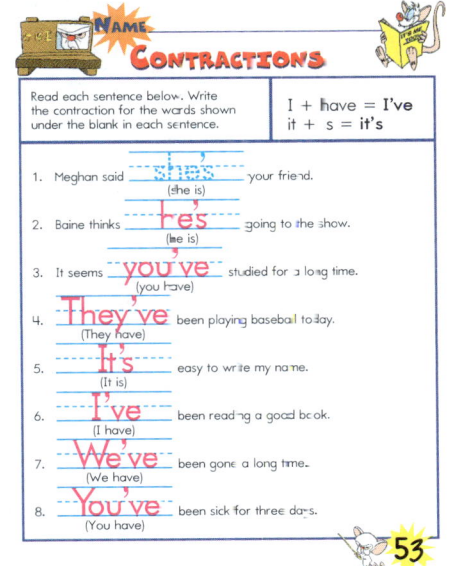
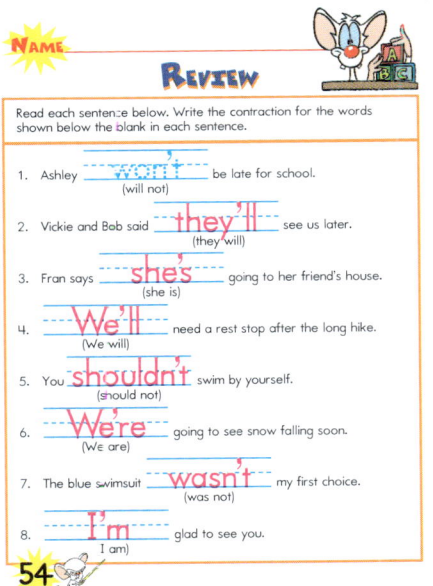
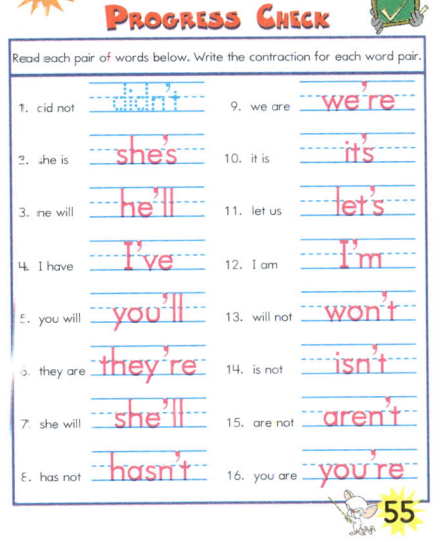
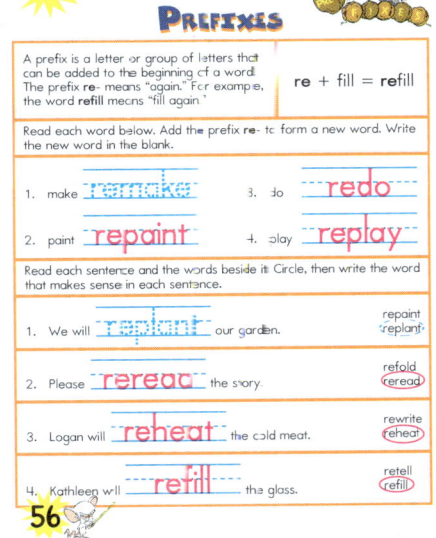

73

Answer Key

 Prefixes

The prefix **un-** means "not" or "the opposite of." For example, the word **unlock** means "the opposite of lock."

un + lock = unlock

Read each word below. Add the prefix **un-** to form a new word. Write the new word in the blank.

1. fair — unfair
2. wrap — unwrap
3. happy — unhappy
4. pack — unpack

Read each sentence and the words beside it. Circle, then write the word that makes sense in each sentence.

1. Will you help me **untie** this knot? — undress / (untie)
2. The little girl looked **unhappy**. — (unhappy) / unlocked
3. Did Andrew **unwrap** his gift yet? — (unwrap) / unfair
4. Mom will **unpack** the box of dishes. — unsafe / (unpack)

57

 Prefixes

Read each sentence and the word beside it. Add **re-** or **un-** to the word to complete each sentence. The word you form must make sense in the sentence.

1. I must **reread** this book. — read
2. Was Paul **unkind** to you? — kind
3. I will **retell** this story. — tell
4. Can you **redraw** the picture? — draw
5. Jeremy must **rewrite** his work. — write
6. The new rule of the game is **unfair**. — fair
7. It is **unwise** to throw away your paper. — wise
8. Driving too fast is **unsafe**. — safe

58

 Suffixes

A suffix is a letter or group of letters that can be added to the end of a word. The suffix **-ful** usually means "full of." For example, the word helpful means "full of help."

play + ful = playful

Read each word below. Add the suffix **-ful** to form a new word. Write the new word in the blank.

1. color — colorful
2. care — careful
3. use — useful
4. pain — painful

Read each sentence and the words beside it. Circle, then write the word that makes sense in each sentence.

1. I was **thankful** to get home. — useful / (thankful)
2. The falling leaves are very **colorful**. — (colorful) / careful
3. My cut hand is **painful**. — playful / (painful)
4. I have a **joyful** smile on my face. — (joyful) / useful

59

 Suffixes

The suffix **-ly** can be added to some words. For example, something done in a **nice** way is done **nicely**.

nice + ly = nicely

Read each word below. Add the suffix **-ly** to form a new word. Write the new word in the blank.

1. soft — softly
2. friend — friendly
3. slow — slowly
4. brave — bravely

Read each sentence and the words beside it. Circle, then write the word that makes sense in each sentence.

1. Dress **warmly** when it is cold. — (warmly) / badly
2. The gloves fit too **tightly**. — (tightly) / slowly
3. The little girl pet the kitten **softly**. — (softly) / nearly
4. Buddy ran **quickly** down the street. — (quickly) / fairly

60

 **Suffixes**

Read each sentence and the word beside it. Add **-ful** or **-ly** to the word to complete each sentence. The word you form must make sense in the sentence.

1. I am **hopeful** of winning the prize. — hope
2. Be sure to write your name **neatly**. — neat
3. Be **careful** when you cross the street. — care
4. Dan plays the horn **loudly**. — loud
5. Joshua **gladly** gave up his turn. — glad
6. Our new puppy is very **playful**. — play
7. I like your **friendly** smile. — friend
8. We study many **useful** things in school. — use

61

Review

Read the list of prefixes and suffixes below. Then add one of the prefixes or suffixes to the underlined word in each group of words. Write the new word in the blank.

re-   un-   -ful   -ly

1. to <u>fill</u> again — refill
2. the opposite of <u>happy</u> — unhappy
3. in a <u>quick</u> way — quickly
4. full of <u>hope</u> — hopeful
5. full of <u>pain</u> — painful
6. in a <u>safe</u> way — safely
7. the opposite of <u>fair</u> — unfair
8. to <u>read</u> again — reread

62

74

Answer Key

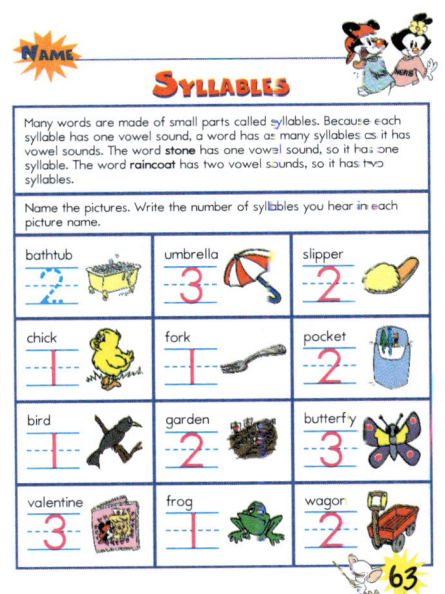

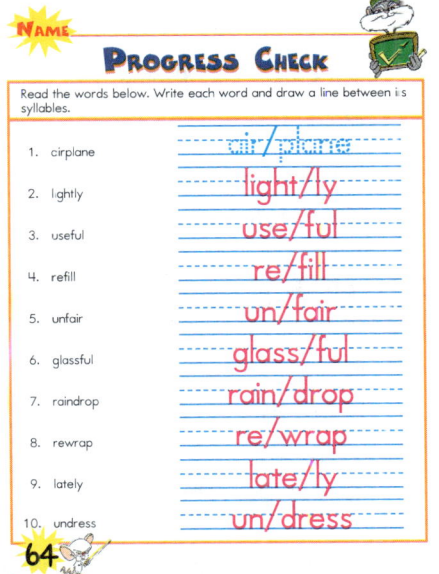

75

Look for all of these entertaining and educational titles in

The McGraw-Hill Junior Academic™ Workbook Series

Toddler

My Colors Go 'Round	ISBN 1-57768-208-4	UPC 6-09746-45118-5
My 1, 2, 3's	ISBN 1-57768-218-1	UPC 6-09746-45128-4
My A, B, C's	ISBN 1-57768-228-9	UPC 6-09746-45138-3
My Ups and Downs	ISBN 1-57768-238-6	UPC 6-09746-45148-2

Preschool

MATH	ISBN 1-57768-209-2	UPC 6-09746-45119-2
READING	ISBN 1-57768-219-X	UPC 6-09746-45129-1
VOWEL SOUNDS	ISBN 1-57768-229-7	UPC 6-09746-45139-0
SOUND PATTERNS	ISBN 1-57768-239-4	UPC 6-09746-45149-9

Kindergarten

MATH	ISBN 1-57768-200-9	UPC 6-09746-45110-9
READING	ISBN 1-57768-210-6	UPC 6-09746-45120-8
PHONICS	ISBN 1-57768-220-3	UPC 6-09746-45130-7
THINKING SKILLS	ISBN 1-57768-230-0	UPC 6-09746-45140-6

Grade 1

MATH	ISBN 1-57768-201-7	UPC 6-09746-45111-6
READING	ISBN 1-57768-211-4	UPC 6-09746-45121-5
PHONICS	ISBN 1-57768-221-1	UPC 6-09746-45131-4
WORD BUILDERS	ISBN 1-57768-231-9	UPC 6-09746-45141-3

Grade 2

MATH	ISBN 1-57768-202-5	UPC 6-09746-45112-3
READING	ISBN 1-57768-212-2	UPC 6-09746-45122-2
PHONICS	ISBN 1-57768-222-X	UPC 6-09746-45132-1
WORD BUILDERS	ISBN 1-57768-232-7	UPC 6-09746-45142-0

Software titles available from
McGRAW-HILL HOME INTERACTIVE

The skills taught in school are now available at home! These titles are now available in retail stores and teacher supply stores everywhere. All titles meet school guidelines and are based on The McGraw-Hill Companies classroom software titles.

MATH GRADES 1 & 2

These math programs are a great way to teach and reinforce skills used in everyday situations. Fun, friendly characters need help with their math skills. Everyone's friend, Nubby the stubby pencil, will help kids master the math in the Numbers Quiz show. Foggy McHammer, a carpenter, needs some help building his playhouse so that all the boards will fit together! Julio Bambino's kitchen antics will surely burn his pastries if you don't help him set the clock timer correctly! We can't forget Turbo Tomato, a fruit with a passion for adventure, who needs help calculating his daredevil stunts.

Math Grades 1 & 2 use a tested, proven approach to reinforcing your child's math skills while keeping him or her intrigued with Nubby and his collection of crazy friends.

TITLE	ISBN	PRICE
Grade 1: Nubby's Quiz Show	1-57768-011-1	$14.95
Grade 2: Foggy McHammer's Treehouse	1-57768-012-X	$14.95

MISSION MASTERS™ MATH AND LANGUAGE ARTS

The Mission Masters™—Pauline, Rakeem, Mia, and T.J.—need your help. The Mission Masters™ are a team of young agents working for the Intelliforce Agency, a high-level cooperative whose goal is to maintain order on our rather unruly planet. From within the agency's top secret Command Control Center, the agency's central computer, M5, has detected a threat...and guess what—you're the agent assigned to the mission!

MISSION MASTERS™ MATH GRADES 3, 4 & 5

This series of exciting activities encourages young mathematicians to challenge themselves and their math skills to overcome the perils of villains and other planetary threats. Skills reinforced include: analyzing and solving real-world problems, estimation, measurements, geometry, whole numbers, fractions, graphs, and patterns.

TITLE	ISBN	PRICE
Grade 3: Mission Masters™ Defeat Dirty D!	1-57768-013-8	$19.95
Grade 4: Mission Masters™ Alien Encounter	1-57768-014-6	$19.95
Grade 5: Mission Masters™ Meet Mudflat Moe	1-57768-015-4	$19.95

MISSION MASTERS™ LANGUAGE ARTS GRADES 3, 4 & 5

This series invites children to apply their language skills to defeat unscrupulous characters and to overcome other earthly dangers. Skills reinforced include: language mechanics and usage, punctuation, spelling, vocabulary, reading comprehension, and creative writing.

TITLE	ISBN	PRICE
Grade 3: Mission Masters™ Freezing Frenzy	1-57768-023-5	$24.95
Grade 4: Mission Masters™ Network Nightmare	1-57768-024-3	$24.95
Grade 5: Mission Masters™ Mummy Mysteries	1-57768-025-1	$24.95

**Look for these and other exciting software titles at a retail store near you.
All titles for Windows 3.1™, Windows '95™, and Macintosh™.
Visit us on the Internet at**

www.MHkids.com

Offers a selection of workbooks to meet all your needs.

Look for all of these fine educational workbooks
in the McGraw-Hill Learning Materials SPECTRUM Series.
All workbooks meet school curriculum guidelines and correspond to
The McGraw-Hill Companies classroom textbooks.

SPECTRUM SERIES

GEOGRAPHY

Full-color, three-part lessons strengthen geography knowledge and map reading skills. Focusing on five geographic themes including location, place, human/environmental interaction, movement, and regions. Over 150 pages. Glossary of geographical terms and answer key included.

TITLE	ISBN	PRICE
Grade 3, Communities	1-57768-153-3	$7.95
Grade 4, Regions	1-57768-154-1	$7.95
Grade 5, USA	1-57768-155-X	$7.95
Grade 6, World	1-57768-156-8	$7.95

MATH

Features easy-to-follow instructions that give students a clear path to success. This series has comprehensive coverage of the basic skills, helping children to master math fundamentals. Over 150 pages. Answer key included.

TITLE	ISBN	PRICE
Grade 1	1-57768-111-8	$6.95
Grade 2	1-57768-112-6	$6.95
Grade 3	1-57768-113-4	$6.95
Grade 4	1-57768-114-2	$6.95
Grade 5	1-57768-115-0	$6.95
Grade 6	1-57768-116-9	$6.95
Grade 7	1-57768-117-7	$6.95
Grade 8	1-57768-118-5	$6.95

PHONICS

Provides everything children need to build multiple skills in language. Focusing on phonics, structural analysis, and dictionary skills, this series also offers creative ideas for using phonics and word study skills in other language arts. Over 200 pages. Answer key included.

TITLE	ISBN	PRICE
Grade K	1-57768-120-7	$6.95
Grade 1	1-57768-121-5	$6.95
Grade 2	1-57768-122-3	$6.95
Grade 3	1-57768-123-1	$6.95
Grade 4	1-57768-124-X	$6.95
Grade 5	1-57768-125-8	$6.95
Grade 6	1-57768-126-6	$6.95

READING

This full-color series creates an enjoyable reading environment, even for below-average readers. Each book contains captivating content, colorful characters, and compelling illustrations, so children are eager to find out what happens next. Over 150 pages. Answer key included.

TITLE	ISBN	PRICE
Grade K	1-57768-130-4	$6.95
Grade 1	1-57768-131-2	$6.95
Grade 2	1-57768-132-0	$6.95
Grade 3	1-57768-133-9	$6.95
Grade 4	1-57768-134-7	$6.95
Grade 5	1-57768-135-5	$6.95
Grade 6	1-57768-136-3	$6.95

SPELLING

This full-color series links spelling to reading and writing and increases skills in words and meanings, consonant and vowel spellings, and proofreading practice. Over 200 pages. Speller dictionary and answer key included.

TITLE	ISBN	PRICE
Grade 1	1-57768-161-4	$7.95
Grade 2	1-57768-162-2	$7.95
Grade 3	1-57768-163-0	$7.95
Grade 4	1-57768-164-9	$7.95
Grade 5	1-57768-165-7	$7.95
Grade 6	1-57768-166-5	$7.95

WRITING

Lessons focus on creative and expository writing using clearly stated objectives and pre-writing exercises. Eight essential reading skills are applied. Activities include main idea, sequence, comparison, detail, fact and opinion, cause and effect, and making a point. Over 130 pages. Answer key included.

TITLE	ISBN	PRICE
Grade 1	1-57768-141-X	$6.95
Grade 2	1-57768-142-8	$6.95
Grade 3	1-57768-143-6	$6.95
Grade 4	1-57768-144-4	$6.95
Grade 5	1-57768-145-2	$6.95
Grade 6	1-57768-146-0	$6.95
Grade 7	1-57768-147-9	$6.95
Grade 8	1-57768-148-7	$6.95

TEST PREP from the Nation's #1 Testing Company

Prepares children to do their best on current editions of the five major standardized tests. Activities reinforce test-taking skills through examples, tips, practice, and timed exercises. Subjects include reading, math, and language. Over 150 pages. Answer key included.

TITLE	ISBN	PRICE
Grade 3	1-57768-103-7	$8.95
Grade 4	1-57768-104-5	$8.95
Grade 5	1-57768-105-3	$8.95
Grade 6	1-57768-106-1	$8.95
Grade 7	1-57768-107-X	$8.95
Grade 8	1-57768-108-8	$8.95

A McGraw·Hill/Warner Bros. Workbook

CERTIFICATE OF ACCOMPLISHMENT

THIS CERTIFIES THAT

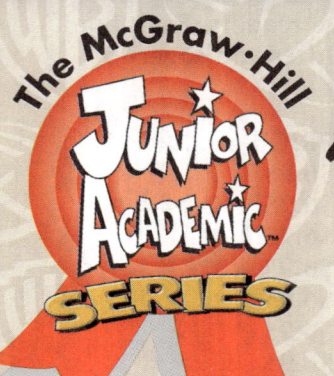

The McGraw·Hill Junior Academic Series

....

HAS SUCCESSFULLY COMPLETED
THE JUNIOR ACADEMIC'S™

Grade 1 Word Builders

WORKBOOK.
CONGRATULATIONS AND THAT'S ALL FOLKS!

Dot & WAKKO Yakko

The McGraw·Hill Companies
PUBLISHER

THE WARNERS—EDITORS-IN-CHIEF

RECEIVE THE McGRAW-HILL PARENT NEWSLETTER

FREE!

Thank you for expressing interest in the successful education of your child. With the purchase of this workbook, we know that you are committed to your child's development and future success. We at **McGraw-Hill Consumer Products** would like to help you make a difference in the education of your child by offering a quarterly newsletter that provides current topics on education and activities that you and your child can work on together.

To receive a free copy of our newsletter, please provide us with the following information:

Name _____

Address _____

City _____ State ____ Zip _____

e-mail (if applicable) _____

Store where book purchased _____

Grade Level of book purchased _____

Title of book purchased _____

Mail to:
Parent Newsletter
c/o McGraw-Hill Consumer Products
251 Jefferson Street, M.S. #12
Waldoboro, ME 04572

Or Call 800-298-4119

Or visit us at:
www.MHkids.com

This offer is limited to residents of the United States and Canada and is only in effect for as long as the newsletter is published.
The information that you provide will not be given, rented, or sold to any company.